The Gospel According to John Cleese

Quotes from the Comic Messiah

SIMON PAIGE

ISBN: 1514162458
ISBN-13: 978-1514162453

DEDICATION

This book is dedicated to The Comic Messiah, John Cleese. Had he not existed it would have been very difficult indeed to find any quotes by him.

CONTENTS

1 INTRODUCTION

In the beginning, God created The Cleese. And God saw The Cleese and thought it was good, and so brought forth The Chapman, Gilliam, Idle, Jones and Palin, and together they became Monty Python.

Monty Python was fruitful and brought joy to many. Seeing this success, The Cleese said, "let there be Fawlty Towers". And so it was. Though the Python had gone its separate ways, The Cleese continued to prosper and subsequently went on to feature on the big screen…

John Cleese has been a genius of comedy for more than 45 years. Throughout this extensive career his unique, dry wit has brought grins and grimaces to many faces, earning him the deserved title of "The Comic Messiah" (courtesy of Mel Smith in *Not The Nine O'Clock News*).

As well as his legendary on-screen status, Cleese is known for his honesty and integrity and has been quoted extensively within the media due to his straight-talking and often controversial opinions.

This book brings together some of the best of Cleese's thoughts on a variety of subjects.

All quotes in this book are words spoken by The Comic Messiah himself.

2 ABOUT MARRIAGE AND HIS DIVORCES

I think marriage should be like dog licences. I think you should have to renew marriage licences every five years, unless you have children. And I think before you have children you should have to go and pass various tests and get a licence to have a child. Because it's the most transformative and difficult thing of your life. Far more important [than work]. People don't understand this, and some people who are highly motivated by work, but when I worked I was always motivated, funnily enough, by the fear of being bad. Because it is so humiliating to make a joke and have no one laugh.

*

Speaking about his divorce from Alyce Faye Eichelberger:

I feel angry sometimes. But my anger is not so much about sharing the property but having to go on working hard to provide alimony for someone who's already going to have at least $10 million worth of property, and who's getting £1 million this year. At some point you say, 'Well, what did I do wrong? You know, I was the breadwinner.' The system is insane.

*

I just think that sometimes we hang onto people or relationships long after they've ceased to be of any use to either of you.

*

On his divorce from Alyce Faye Eichelberger:

This is the happiest I have ever been and I feel that at 68 now I want as many years as I can get.

*

Speaking further about the same divorce:

We broke up in the marital therapist's office. We'd been
seeing them for a couple of years. And we agreed to break
up and three weeks later I heard about the lawyer that she
was using and I rang her up and said, 'Do you know this
lawyer's reputation?' And she said, 'I hear that yours can be
pretty nasty, too.' And I said, 'OK, here's an offer. You get
rid of yours. I'll get rid of mine. I'll appoint someone
you're comfortable with, you appoint someone I'm
comfortable with and it could be fairly easy.' And she said,
'No, I'm not interested. I would like to stay with the
present situation.'

*

When I got divorced from Connie Booth, with whom I
had dinner on Sunday, and when I got divorced from
Barbara Trentham, I didn't need lawyers on either
occasion, because I just sort of said, 'Why don't I give you
this?' And they said, 'That's very fair, very generous. Thank
you.' End of story. This woman [Alyce Faye Eichelberger]
now was asking my old St John's Wood accountants for 60
boxes of documents, so many documents that they had to
send people out from California to go through them.

*

The divorce settlement absolutely affects every decision I make professionally. I have to earn $1 million a year before I even get to keep a penny and I have to build my professional choices around that fact. It annoys me that in my seventies I am having to live in a way I don't choose to live. Imagine how much I'd have had to pay Alyce if she had contributed anything to the relationship - such as children or a conversation.

*

When Alyce had her hip replacement I realised that there was a chance for a little humour and I sent a bunch of flowers to her lawyer's office saying, "Would you please inspect these flowers and see whether they are acceptable and would you please vet the greetings card that comes with these and see whether that is also legitimate. And if you are satisfied that both of them are not harmful, would you be good enough to send them on to my wife as soon as possible?" To which the lawyer replied: "As the trade papers say, he's not as funny as he was." The sort of leaden, nasty - what's the word? - black-hearted response to a little conceit.

3 ABOUT HIMSELF

Don't let anyone tell you what you ought to like... Some wines that some experts think are absolutely exquisite don't appeal to me at all.

*

I'm probably the worst singer in Europe. I won't compete for North America.

*

I'm always meeting new people, and my list of friends seems to change quite a bit.

*

I don't want to have to start being unselfish again. The great thing about being on your own is you do what you damn well like.

*

The one thing I remember about Christmas was that my father used to take me out in a boat about ten miles offshore on Christmas Day, and I used to have to swim back. Extraordinary. It was a ritual. Mind you, that wasn't the hard part. The difficult bit was getting out of the sack.

*

Most of the bad taste I've been accused of has been generic bad taste; it's been making fun of an idea as opposed to a person.

*

When I was a child and I was upset about something, my mother was not capable of containing that emotion, of letting me be upset but reassuring me, of just being with me in a calming way. She always got in a flap, so I not only had my own baby panics, fears and terrors to deal with, but I had to cope with hers, too. Eventually I taught myself to remain calm when I was panicked, in order not to upset her. In a way, she had managed to put me in charge of her. At 18 months old, I was doing the parenting.

*

Technology frightens me to death. It's designed by engineers to impress other engineers. And they always come with instruction booklets that are written by engineers for other engineers — which is why almost no technology ever works.

*

I can do anything I want, I'm eccentric!

*

I was always a sports nut but I've lost interest now in whether one bunch of mercenaries in north London is going to beat another bunch of mercenaries from west London.

*

Speaking about moving from England to California:

At my age, I want to wake up and see sunshine pouring in through the windows every day.

*

I always felt attracted by Austrian and German culture in a certain way. I've always liked Vienna. I never saw so much theatre and music and so many museums anywhere else. I like the city's velocity and the food. It doesn't have the tackiness of other big cities. I considered renting a small flat in Switzerland. I love being in Lyon, Strasbourg, Munich and Milan in four hours from there.

*

I used to desire many, many things, but now I have just one desire, and that's to get rid of all my other desires.

*

It's very important for me that my friends have a sense of humour. To me it's the kind of touchstone of communication. Alyce Faye Eichelberger's sense of humour was not very European, because she was from Oklahoma and I used to joke that the Oklahoma Sense of Irony is one of the world's short books.

*

I had a very, very difficult relationship with my mother, who was supremely self-centred. She was hilariously self-centred. She did not really take interest in anything that didn't immediately affect her.

*

For me, the great problem growing up in England was that I had a very narrow concept of what God can be, and it was damn close to an old man with a beard.

*

My mum died about three years ago at the age of 101, and just towards the end, as she began to run out of energy, she did actually stop trying to tell me what to do most of the time.

*

I don't miss London much. I find it crowded, vast and difficult to get around. Cabs are incredibly expensive.

*

If I can get you to laugh with me, you like me better, which makes you more open to my ideas. And if I can persuade you to laugh at the particular point I make, by laughing at it you acknowledge its truth.

*

I would say that I began with a very edgy, very driven personality and after a sufficient amount of therapy over many, many years, I managed to become rather relaxed and happy.

*

I have several times made a poor choice by avoiding a necessary confrontation.

*

Sci-fi has never really been my bag. But I do believe in a lot of weird things these days, such as synchronicity. Quantum physics suggests it's possible, so why not?

*

I was asked to do a reality show a few months ago. I forget which one it was, it might have been the jungle one or perhaps Celebrity Root Canal. I just laughed, then asked how much they were offering out of curiosity. It was £200,000, but I would never agree to one of those shows. That would mean the collapse of western civilization. There is always a filter when it comes to accepting work. I call it the EQ - the embarrassment quota. I will only do embarrassing things if there is a lot of money involved and people won't really know about it.

*

Talking about why he had to avoid living in London during the 2012 Olympics:

I'm in a very strange situation. Because of the tax situation in the UK and because I have to pay this enormous alimony every year of one million dollars, I discovered that if I live in London, which I was intending to do, I have to make two million dollars before I keep a penny. That's quite a lot. So I'm not going to be living in London. The result of that for at least a year, I'm hardly allowed to go back there at all. (On why he has to avoid living in London during the 2012 Summer Olympics)

*

I had a very, very difficult relationship with my mother, who was supremely self-centred. She was hilariously self-centred. She did not really take interest in anything that didn't immediately affect her.

*

I don't miss London much. I find it crowded, vast and difficult to get around. Cabs are incredibly expensive.

4 PHILOSOPHY, POLITICS AND RELIGION

I think that money spoils most things, once it becomes the
primary motivating force.

*

He who laughs most, learns best.

*

A wonderful thing about true laughter is that it just destroys any kind of system of dividing people.

*

A man will give up almost anything except his suffering.

*

God was treated like this powerful, erratic, rather punitive father who has to be pacified and praised. You know, flattered.

*

Acting is all about faking. We're all very good at faking things that we have no competence with.

*

You don't have to be the Dalai Lama to tell people that
life's about change.

*

I think that the real religion is about the understanding that
if we can only still our egos for a few seconds, we might
have a chance of experiencing something that is divine in
nature. But in order to do that, we have to slice away at
our egos and try to get them down to a manageable size,
and then still work some practiced light meditation. So real
religion is about reducing our egos, whereas all the
churches are interested in is egotistical activities, like
getting as many members and raising as much money and
becoming as important and high-profile and influential as
possible. All of which are egotistical attitudes. So how can
you have an egotistical organization trying to teach a non-
egotistical ideal? It makes no sense, unless you regard
religion as crowd control. What I think most organized
religion—simply crowd control.

*

I'm not saying Obama is right on everything. Of course not. He may be wrong on a number of things. But what I do know is that he behaves like a very, very sane man almost all the time.

*

Creativity is not a talent. It is a way of operating.

*

Too many people confuse being serious with being solemn.

*

Nothing will stop you being creative more effectively as
the fear of making a
mistake.

*

Laughter is a force for democracy.

*

I think that money spoils most things, once it becomes the
primary motivating force.

*

This is the extraordinary thing about creativity: If just you keep your mind resting against the subject in a friendly but persistent way, sooner or later you will get a reward from your unconscious.

*

I think there's much more fear now than there used to be, much more fear of failure.

*

When people say "I'm not a prude, but..." what they mean is "I am a prude, and..."

5 GENERAL HUMOUR

If God did not intend for us to eat animals, then why did
he make them out of meat?

*

Why anyone who has not committed a punishable offence
would listen to country and western music is beyond me.

*

Oh, I could spend my life having this conversation - look - please try to understand before one of us dies.

*

Life is a terminal disease, and it is sexually transmitted.

*

Why write about the past? Well, there's more of it.

*

Someone telephonically knowledgeable and I had a bit of an argument about that. He said that telephone booths didn't work because they were vandalized. I said they were vandalized because they didn't work.

*

I don't think anyone should be educated sexually. There's far too many people on the planet. If we could hush it up for a few years, that would help.

*

If you wish to kill yourself but lack the courage to, I think a visit to Palmerston North will do the trick.

6 ABOUT HIS WORK

My compulsion to always be working has become less strong and my current business is purely down to this enormous alimony. If I wasn't doing this I'd be making documentaries about wildlife and other subjects that interest me.

*

The really good idea is always traceable back quite a long way, often to a not very good idea which sparked off another idea that was only slightly better, which somebody else misunderstood in such a way that they then said something which was really rather interesting.

*

The Americans all love 'The Holy Grail', and the English all love 'Life Of Brian', and I'm afraid on this one, I side with the English.

*

Filming takes a lot out of you. It really does. It's immensely demanding, and you have to put the rest of your life in the icebox until you do your final shot.

*

When you've been doing comedy for forty years, you really do know most of the jokes. And even if you don't know a specific joke, you can pretty much guess what it's going to be.

*

I tend to have an odd split in my mind: I tend to look at it as a writer and when the writing thing is OK and I'm happy with it, then I put on my actor's hat.

*

Speaking about Fawlty Towers:

There is a famous note which I have a copy of, I think it's framed. What happened was, Connie and I wrote that first episode and we sent it in to Jimmy Gilbert (James Gilbert). And first of all the fellow whose job it was to assess the quality of the writing said, and I can quote it fairly accurately, "This is full of clichéd situations and stereotypical characters and I cannot see it as being anything other than a disaster". And Jimmy himself said "You're going to have to get them out of the hotel, John, you can't do the whole thing in the hotel". Whereas, of course, it's in the hotel that the whole pressure cooker builds up.

*

I can't tell you how scary it can be walking onto a movie and suddenly joining this family, it's like going to somebody else's Christmas dinner, everyone knows everyone, and you're there and you're not quite sure what you're supposed to be doing.

*

I find it rather easy to portray a businessman. Being bland, rather cruel and incompetent comes naturally to me.

*

Who's ever going to write a film in which I get the girl? Me!

*

About Monty Python:

I think that sometimes you do something that makes a small group of people laugh, which is all we were trying to do; we were just trying to make each other laugh.

*

Filming is like a long air journey: there's so much hanging around and boredom that they keep giving you food.

*

I never enjoyed "The Meaning of Life". I always regarded that entire film as a bit of a cockup.

*

I think you can write very good comedy without a partner, but what I love about it, working with a partner, is that you get to places you'd never get on your own. It's like when God was designing the world and decided we couldn't have children without a partner; it was a way of mixing up the genes so you'd get a more interesting product.

*

I can never do better than Fawlty Towers whatever I do. Now I very much want to teach young talent some rules of the game.

*

Talking about the Daniel Craig Bond films:

I did two James Bond movies and then I believe that they decided that the tone they needed was that of the Bourne action movies, which are very gritty and humorless. Also, the big money was coming from Asia, from the Philippines, Vietnam, Indonesia, where the audiences go to watch the action sequences, and that's why in my opinion the action sequences go on for too long, and it's a fundamental flaw. The audiences in Asia are not going for the subtle British humor or the class jokes.

*

Most of the bad taste I've been accused of has been generic bad taste; it's been making fun of an idea as opposed to a person. Oddly enough, the one or two jokes I really regret on Python are the more personal ones. We did have this thing about David Hemmings ... something about him being played by a piece of wood. At the end there was a voice-over saying: "David Hemmings appeared by permission of the Forestry Commission." Afterwards, I felt just a little bit guilty.

*

Speaking about making commercials during the writing of Fawlty Towers:

I have to thank the advertising industry for making this possible. Connie and I used to spend six weeks writing each episode and we didn't make a lot of money out of it.

If it hadn't been for the commercials I wouldn't have been able to afford to spend so much time on the script.

*

Comedy always works best when it is mean-spirited.

*

Well, the only way I can get a leading-man role is if I write it.

*

Some people ask me to do ads and I think, I don't really want to sell potato crisps.

7 ABOUT THE TELEVISION AND FILM INDUSTRY

Speaking about British television:

I don't think the writers work as hard as they used to, and I think they may lack experience because I don't think the writing is as good as it used to be. But I do proudly say that in the 60s, 70s and 80s we did have the least bad television in the world, and that's quite a claim. I think the main problem now is it's run on the basis of money.

*

Speaking in 2013 about the BBC:

The people who became executives [in the Sixties and Seventies] had produced or directed a great deal of comedy. Now there seems to be an executive class and they have never written and never directed.

*

Some actors, I think, want to feel that they are as creative as the writer. And the answer is, frankly, they're not.

*

When the target audience is American teenage kids, you can have problems. My generation prized really fine acting and writing. Sometimes you have to go back to the basic principles which underpin great visual comedy.

*

It's lovely that Harry Potter and the Bond movies are still shot in England - that's a great pleasure, but it's true that most of the well-paid work is in America.

*

You go in and meet the head of BBC One and get an assurance about not dumbing down. And then, of course a few months later, he's been replaced by someone you haven't met.

*

English television from the Fifties to the Nineties was the least bad in the world, and now it's just as bad as it is anywhere.

*

Movie executives have almost no idea what they're doing. In fact, I would say that's an incorrect statement. I would say the executives don't have ANY idea what they're doing. But they don't have any idea that they have no idea, so they're blundering around. They're trying to control everything without having a clue what's really going on. And that's very sad because if somebody put me in charge of BBC comedy, I could resurrect it in six months. At the moment, the people there are just very poor.

*

When I was growing up, we had the best television in the world. Now it's as bad as it is everywhere else, and I don't particularly want to participate in that. I don't really watch TV these days, except live sport. There's nothing much that appeals to me and I would rather read a book.

8 ABOUT OTHER PEOPLE

I was very sad to hear of the death of Ronnie Barker, who
was such a warm, friendly and encouraging presence to
have when I started in television. He was also a great
comic actor to learn from.

*

Part of the eulogy he gave at Graham Chapman's
memorial service:

Graham Chapman, co-author of the "Parrot Sketch", is no
more. He has ceased to be. Bereft of life, he rests in peace.
He's kicked the bucket, hopped the twig, bit the dust,
snuffed it, breathed his last, and gone to meet the great
Head of Light Entertainment in the sky. And I guess that
we're all thinking how sad it is that a man of such talent, of
such capability for kindness, of such unusual intelligence,
should now so suddenly be spirited away at the age of only
forty-eight, before he'd achieved many of the things of
which he was capable, and before he'd had enough fun.
Well, I feel that I should say: nonsense. Good riddance to
him, the freeloading bastard, I hope he fries. And the
reason I feel I should say this is he would never forgive me
if I didn't, if I threw away this glorious opportunity to
shock you all on his behalf. Anything for him but mindless
good taste.

(He then paused for a second and claimed that Chapman
had whispered in his ear while he was writing the speech):

All right, Cleese. You say you're very proud of being the
very first person ever to say 'shit' on British television. If
this service is really for me, just for starters, I want you to
become the first person ever at a British memorial service
to say 'fuck'.

*

Talking about Russell Brand and Jonathan Ross' phone call to Andrew Sachs (who played Manuel in Fawlty Towers) live on air:

I think that phone call was astoundingly tasteless. Apparently Russell Brand had actually slept with the girl, who works in a slightly raunchy club. Oh yes, a burlesque club. Anyway ... I can't imagine why they would ring Andrew up. It was, as I say, very tasteless. I thought that was extraordinary, especially as I've met Jonathan Ross and liked him; it's very hard to see why he would have done it.

*

Michael Palin decided to give up on his considerable comedy talents to make those dreadfully tedious travel shows. Have you ever tried to watch one?

*

The thrill I got discovering Buster Keaton when I was growing up was so exciting. He was one of the greats.

*

Speaking again about Jonathon Ross' obscene phone call
to Andrew Sachs:

I'm uneasy about censorship so I think that it's important
to hire people who have good enough taste to censor
themselves. I've always thought that Jonathan Ross would
have fallen into this category.

*

If life were fair, Dan Quayle would be making a living
asking "Do you want fries with that?"

*

In the early days of my career, I'd have these moments of utter delight: at the age of 21, I discovered Buster Keaton; at 24 it was Harold Lloyd; then W.C. Fields. Just occasionally, one discovers someone new for oneself. I thought Bill Hicks was a genius, Eddie Izzard too. I don't want to be mean but there are several highly regarded shows around right now - and I'm not talking about Ricky Gervais, because I think he's excellent - that I don't much care for. So basically I keep my mouth shut. At this stage of my life I have to accept that I'm not likely to come across anything as startlingly good as Buster Keaton.

*

Although my inclinations are slightly left-of-center, I was terribly disappointed with the last Labour government. Gordon Brown lacked emotional intelligence and was never a leader.

9 OTHER NOTABLE QUOTES

The most creative people have this childlike facility to play.

*

It seems astounding to me now that the video games are perhaps as important as the movie themselves. And people will spend 2 or 3 years obsessing about the video game in exactly the same way that they'd be obsessing about the movie if they were working on that.

*

If you want creative workers, give them enough time to play.

*

In Britain, girls seem to be either bright or attractive. In America, that's not the case. They're both.

*

Because, as we all know, it's easier to do trivial things that are urgent than it is to do important things that are not urgent, like thinking. And it's also easier to do little things we know we can do than to start on big things that we're not so sure about.

*

We don't know where we get our ideas from. What we do know is that we do not get them from our laptops.

*

Now most people do not want an ordinary life in which they do a job well, earn the respect of their collaborators and competitors, bring up a family and have friends. That's not enough any more, and I think that is absolutely tragic - and I'm not exaggerating - that people feel like a decent, ordinary, fun life is no longer enough.

*

The English contribution to world cuisine - the chip.

*

I think it's because in America you always get the sense that if you fail, you can just pack up your things and go somewhere else and try again. But in England, it's so geographically small that if somebody succeeds here, it reduces your chances of succeeding.

*

Wine is wonderful stuff. But so many people are put off by the snobbery of it.

*

England changed much more than I did. We used to have some sort of middle class culture with an adequate amount of respect for education. It was a bit racist - not in a mean way though, but still racist. Some things have changed for the better. But it's not a middle class culture anymore, but a yob culture, a rowdy culture.

*

England is a fairly envious little country and it's embodied
in the press. They don't like anyone being more
distinguished than they are.

*

The thing you have to remember about critics is that they
can't do it themselves.

*

I think the problem with people like this is that they are so
stupid that they have no idea how stupid they are.

*

I love having different cultures around, but when the parent culture kind of dissipates, you're left thinking, "Well, what's going on?"

*

In Britain, girls seem to be either bright or attractive. In America, that's not the case. They're both.

ABOUT THE AUTHOR

Simon Paige is a very silly man who writes very silly books and very silly articles on the internet. He is also a fond admirer of very silly comedy.

Made in the USA
Coppell, TX
10 October 2020